HANDWITING

LEARN TO PRINT!

stanfordpub.com

Name
Grade

1
3
2
1
2
3
Trace and write the letters:

B b
1
2
3
4
Trace and write the letters:

Cc
Trace and write the letters:

Dd
Trace and write the letters:

Trace and write the letters:

Trace and write the letters:

Trace and write the letters:

Hh

Trace and write the letters:

H H H H H H H H H H H H

H H H

H

h h h h h h h h h h h h

h h h

h

Ll
Li
Trace and write the letters:

1
2
1
2
Trace and write the letters:

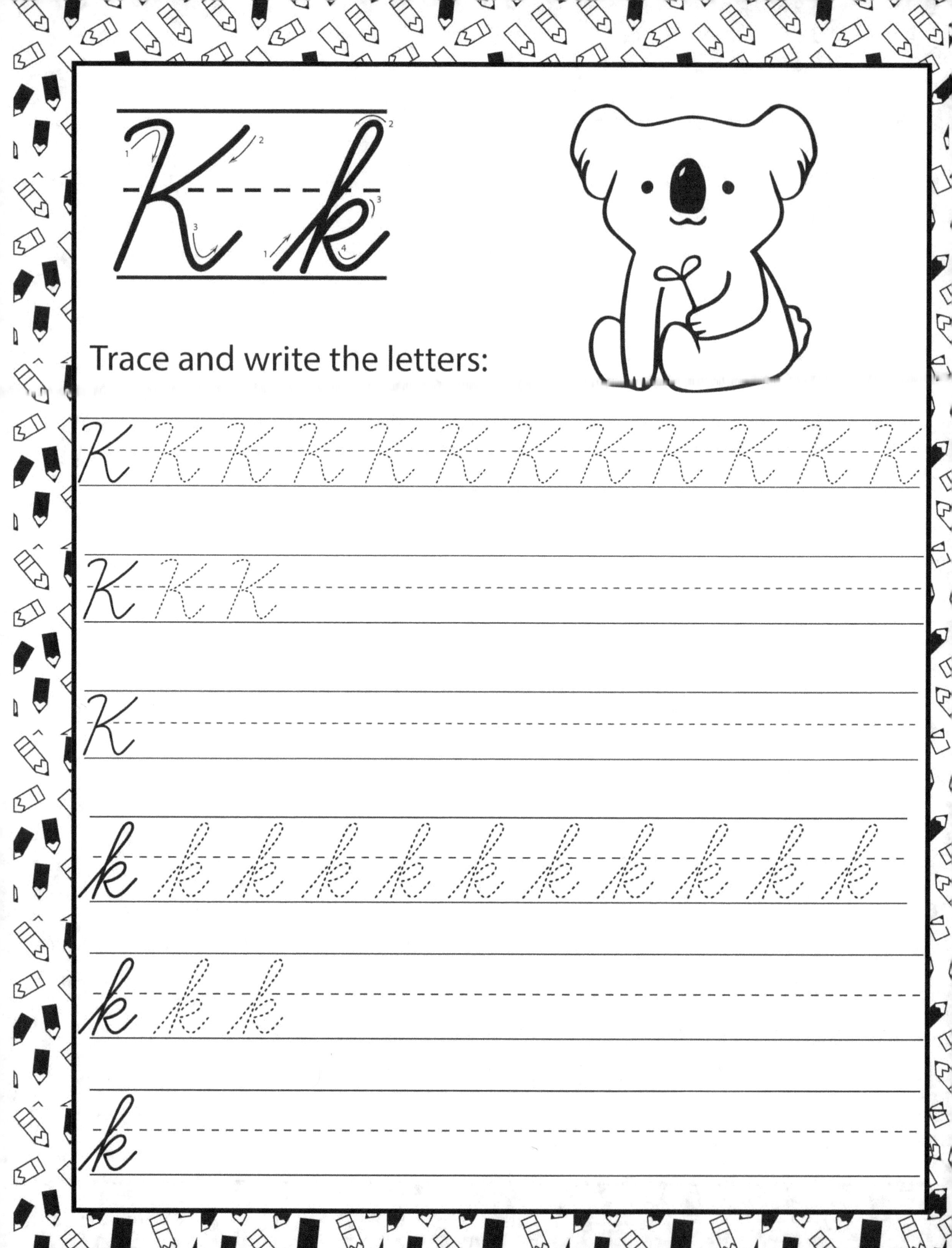
Kk
Trace and write the letters:

Trace and write the letters:

Mm
Trace and write the letters:

Nn

Trace and write the letters:

N N N N N N N N N N N N

N N N

N

n n n n n n n n n n

n n n

n

Trace and write the letters:

Trace and write the letters:

Q q
1
2
1
2
3
4
5
Trace and write the letters:

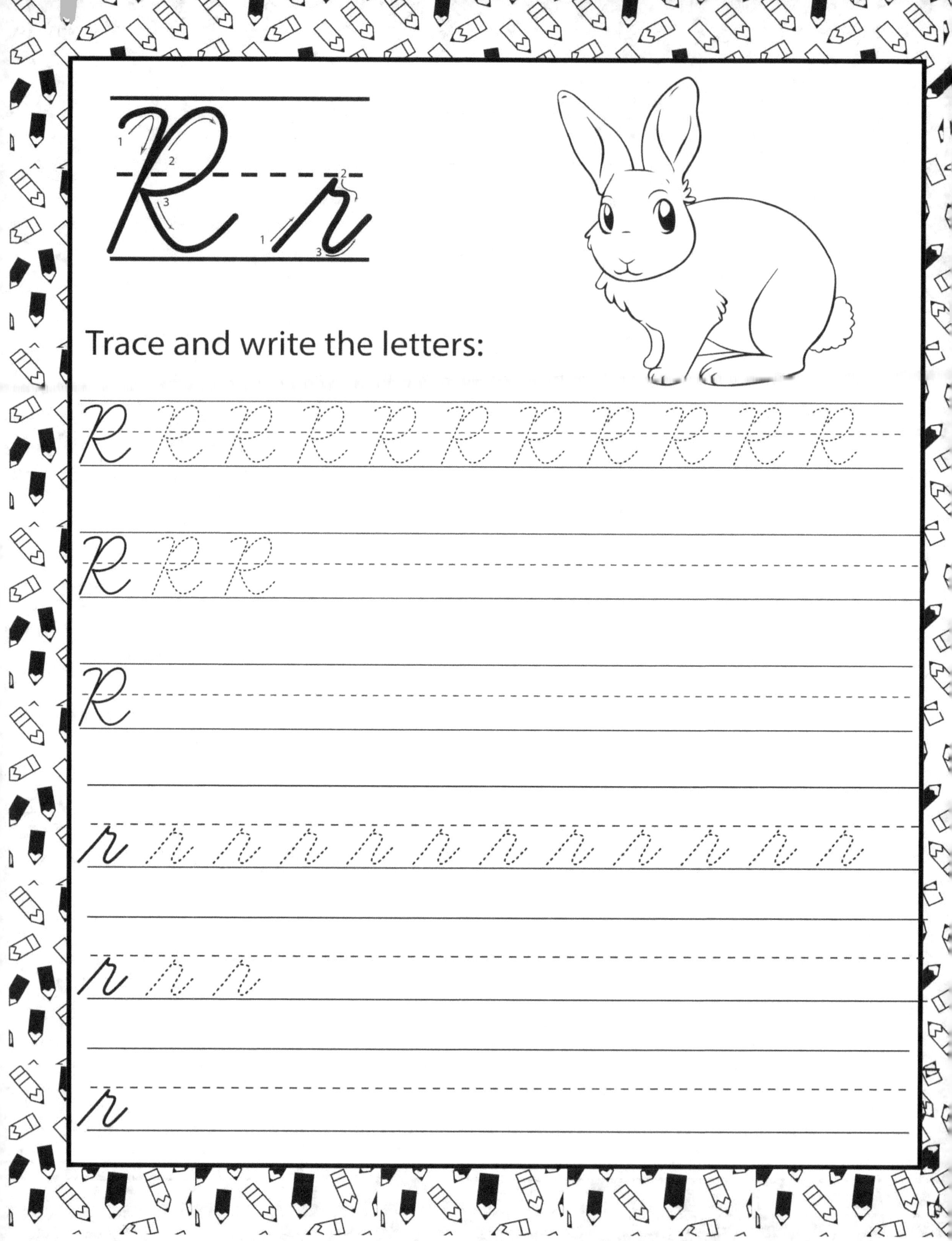
Rr
1
2
3
1
2
3
Trace and write the letters:
R R R R R R R R R R R
R R R
R
r r r r r r r r r r r r
r r r
r

Trace and write the letters:

Tt
Trace and write the letters:

Trace and write the letters:

Trace and write the letters:

Ww
Trace and write the letters:

Trace and write the letters:

Yy
Trace and write the letters:

1
2
1
2
Trace and write the letters:

Cursive Letter Joins Worksheets

Trace and write the letters:

ai ai ai ai ai ai ai ai ai ai

ai ai ai

ai ai ai

ai ai

ai

ar
Trace and write the letters:
ar ar ar ar ar ar ar ar ar ar
ar ar ar
ar ar ar
ar ar
ar

Trace and write the letters:

au au au au au au au au

au au au

au au au

au au

au

aw
Trace and write the letters:
aw aw aw aw aw aw aw
aw aw aw
aw aw aw
aw aw
aw

ay
Trace and write the letters:
ay ay ay ay ay ay ay ay
ay ay ay
ay ay ay
ay ay
ay

Trace and write the letters:

ck
Trace and write the letters:
ck ck ck ck ck ck ck ck ck ck
ck ck ck
ck ck ck
ck ck
ck

er

Trace and write the letters:

er er er er er er er er er er er

er er er

er er er

er er

er

Trace and write the letters:

ew
Trace and write the letters:
ew ew ew ew ew ew ew ew
ew ew ew
ew ew ew
ew ew
ew

ir
Trace and write the letters:
ir
ir
ir
ir
ir

kn

Trace and write the letters:

kn *kn* *kn* *kn* *kn* *kn* *kn* *kn*

kn *kn* *kn*

kn *kn* *kn*

kn *kn*

kn

as
Trace and write the letters:
as as as as as as as as a as
as as as
as as as
as as
as

ea

Trace and write the letters:

ea *ea* *ea* *ea* *ea* *ea* *ea* *ea* *ea* *ea*

ea *ea* *ea*

ea *ea* *ea*

ea *ea*

ea

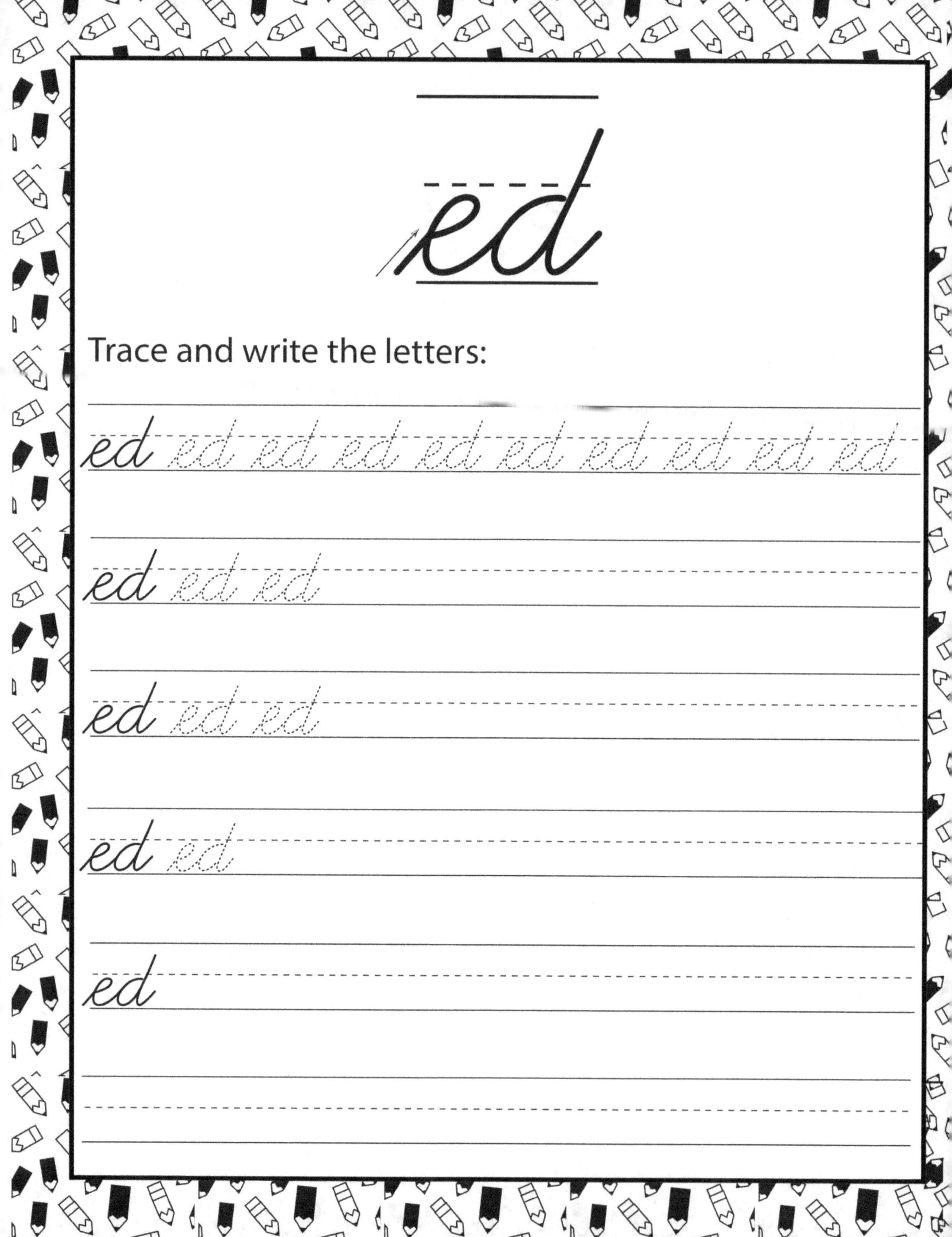
ed
Trace and write the letters:
ed ed ed ed ed ed ed ed ed ed
ed ed ed
ed ed ed
ed ed
ed

Ss
Trace and write the letters:
Ss
Ss
Ss
Ss
Ss

igh
Trace and write the letters:
igh igh igh igh igh igh igh
igh igh igh
igh igh igh
igh igh
igh

ing
Trace and write the letters:
ing ing ing ing ing ing
ing ing ing
ing ing ing
ing ing
ing

squ

Trace and write the letters:

squ squ squ squ squ squ squ

squ squ squ

squ squ squ

squ squ

squ

Cursive Words Worksheets

Aa

1 3 2 1 2 3

Trace and write the letters:

Asia Asia

also also

aunt aunt

apple apple

anger anger

ankle ankle

B b

Trace and write the letters:

Boston Boston

bee bee

busy busy

bottom bottom

blue blue

broken broken

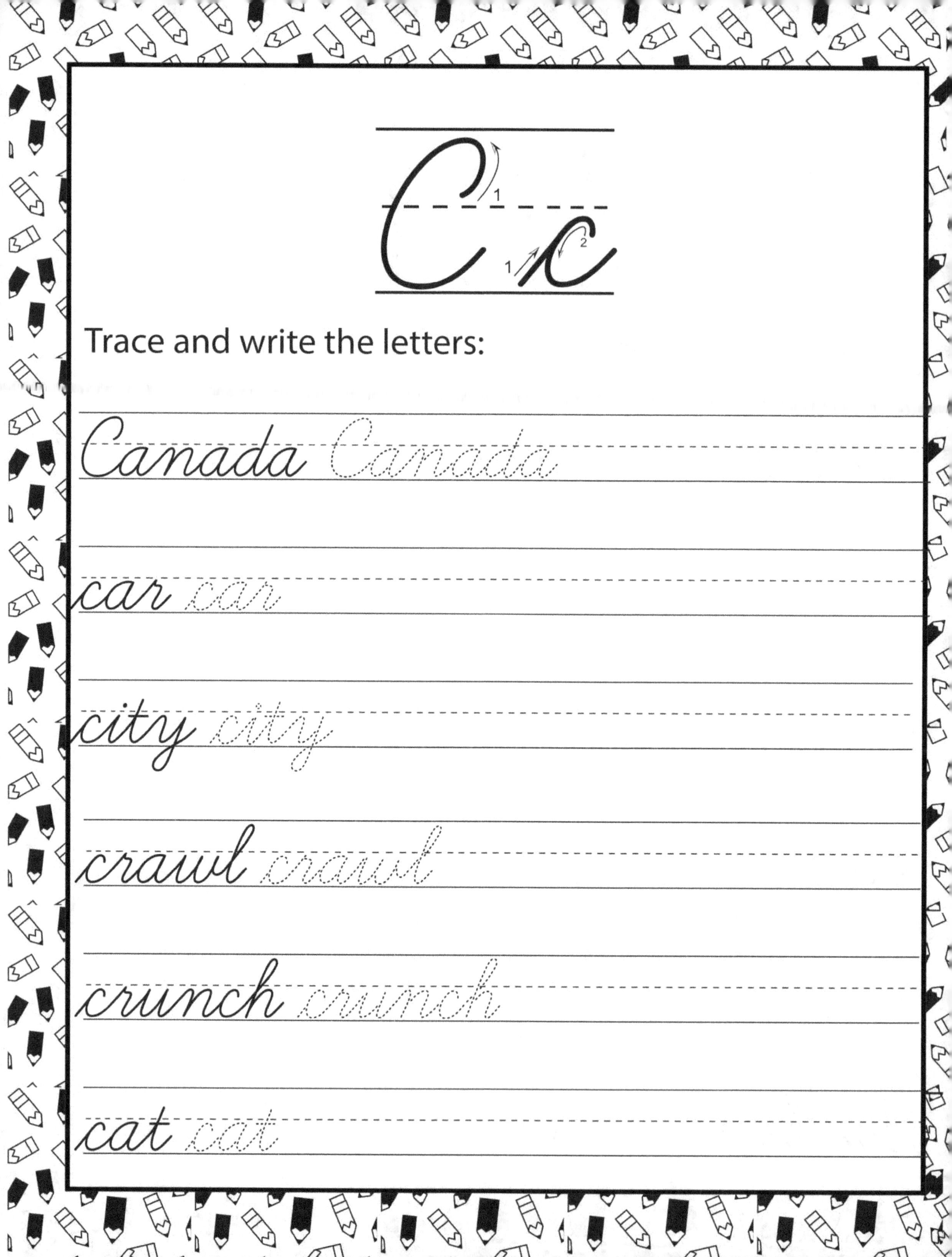

Cc

Trace and write the letters:

Canada Canada

car car

city city

crawl crawl

crunch crunch

cat cat

Dd

Trace and write the letters:

drive drive

door door

don't don't

David David

dish dish

dog dog

Ee
1
2
3
1
2
3
Trace and write the letters:
egg egg
edge edge
everyone everyone
ear ear
Earth Earth
early early

Ff

Trace and write the letters:

fire fire

flow flow

friend friend

family family

feather feather

Florence Florence

Gg

Trace and write the letters:

grand grand

George George

get get

going going

girl girl

giving giving

Hh

1 2 3 4 1 2 3

Trace and write the letters:

hand hand

Harrison Harrison

he's he's

hat hat

heart heart

house house

I i
1
2
1
2
Trace and write the letters:
idea idea
inch inch
isn't isn't
icing icing
iron iron
Iowa Iowa

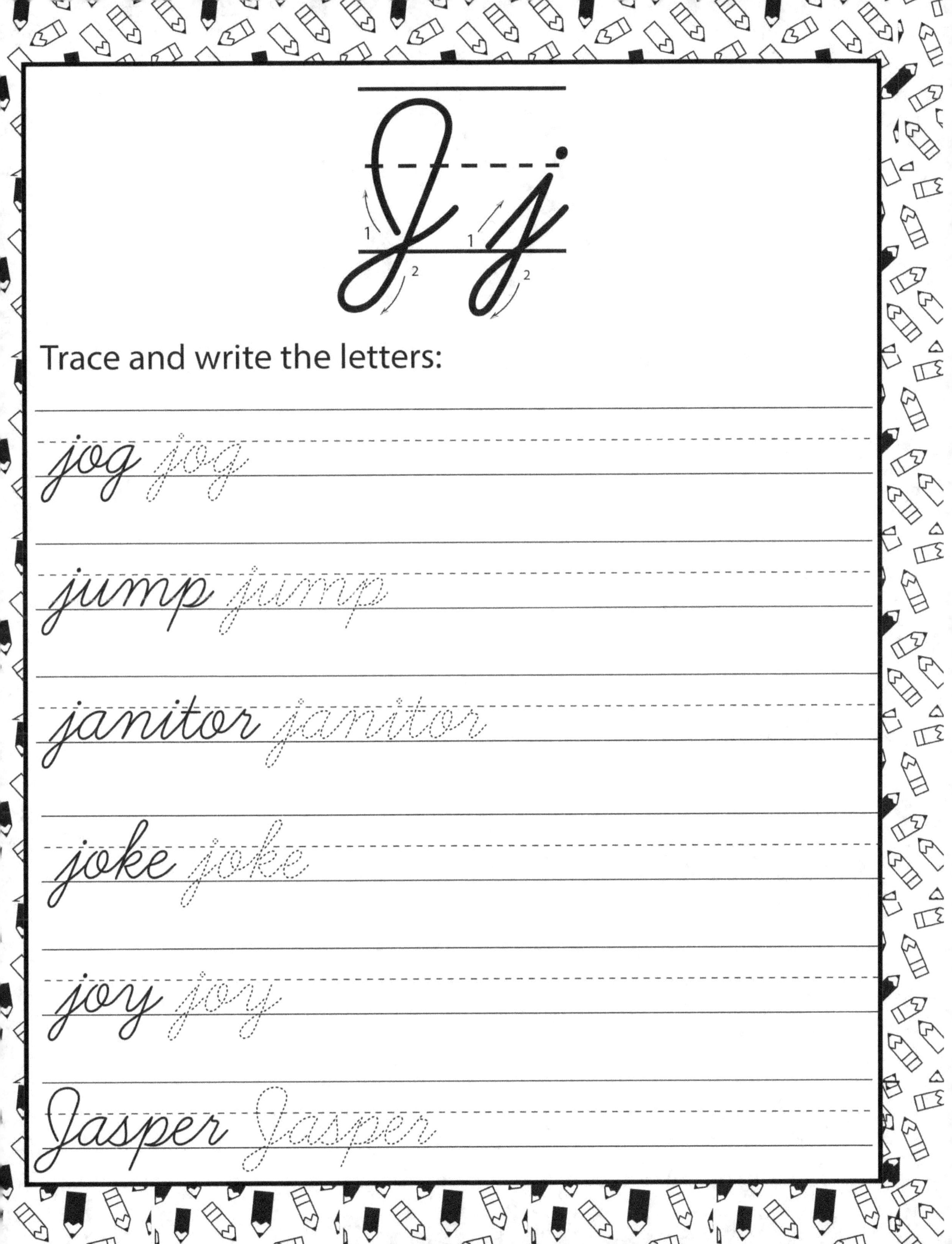

Jj
1
2
1
2
Trace and write the letters:
jog jog
jump jump
janitor janitor
joke joke
joy joy
Jasper Jasper

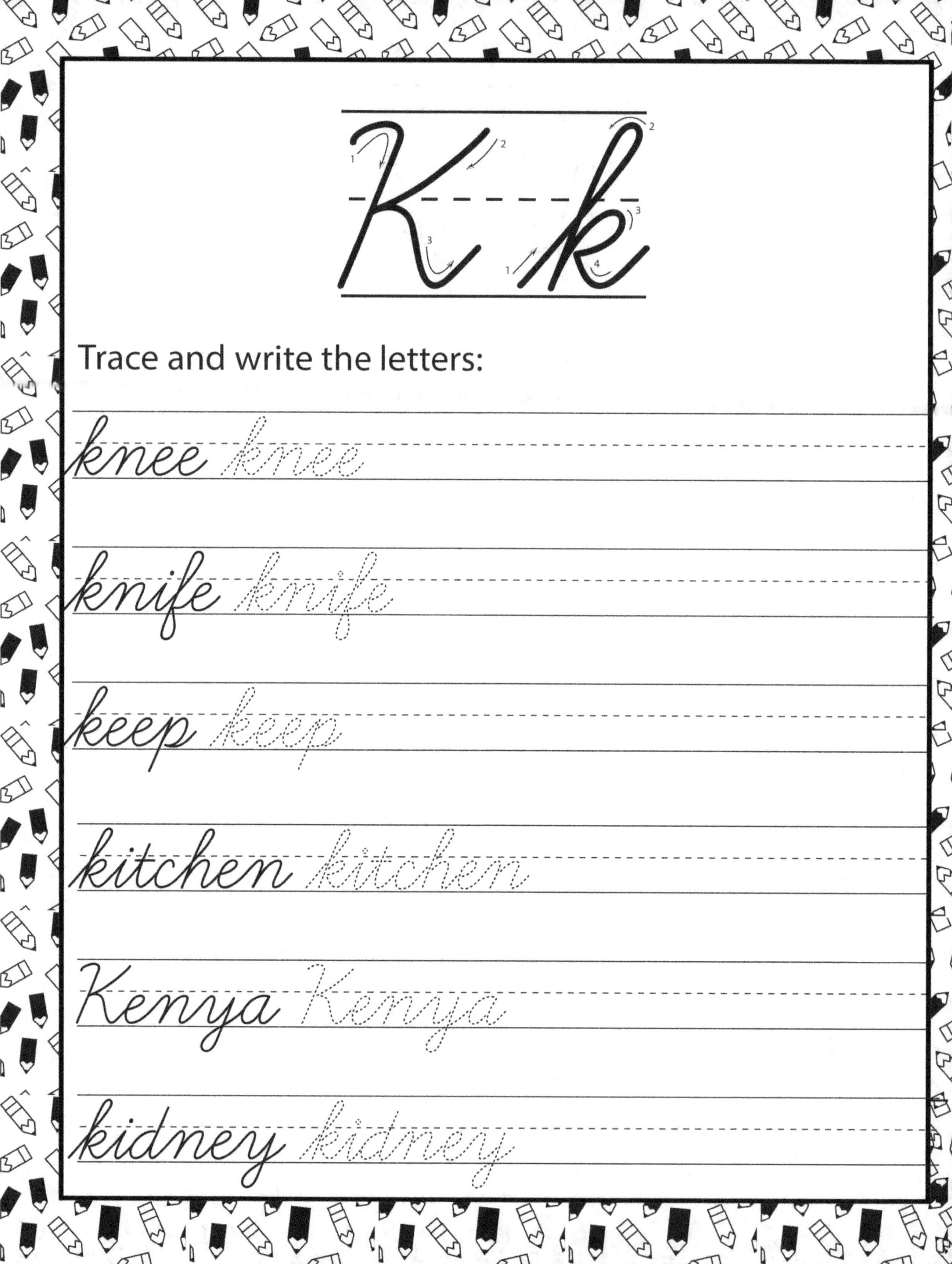
Kk
Trace and write the letters:
knee knee
knife knife
keep keep
kitchen kitchen
Kenya Kenya
kidney kidney

L l

1 2 2 3 1 3

Trace and write the letters:

love love

life life

lawn lawn

light light

Lakeside Lakeside

lucky lucky

Mm

1 2 3 1 2 3

Trace and write the letters:

map map

mother mother

must must

Maine Maine

monday monday

morning morning

Nn

Trace and write the letters:

Newport Newport

need need

night night

neck neck

neat neat

number number

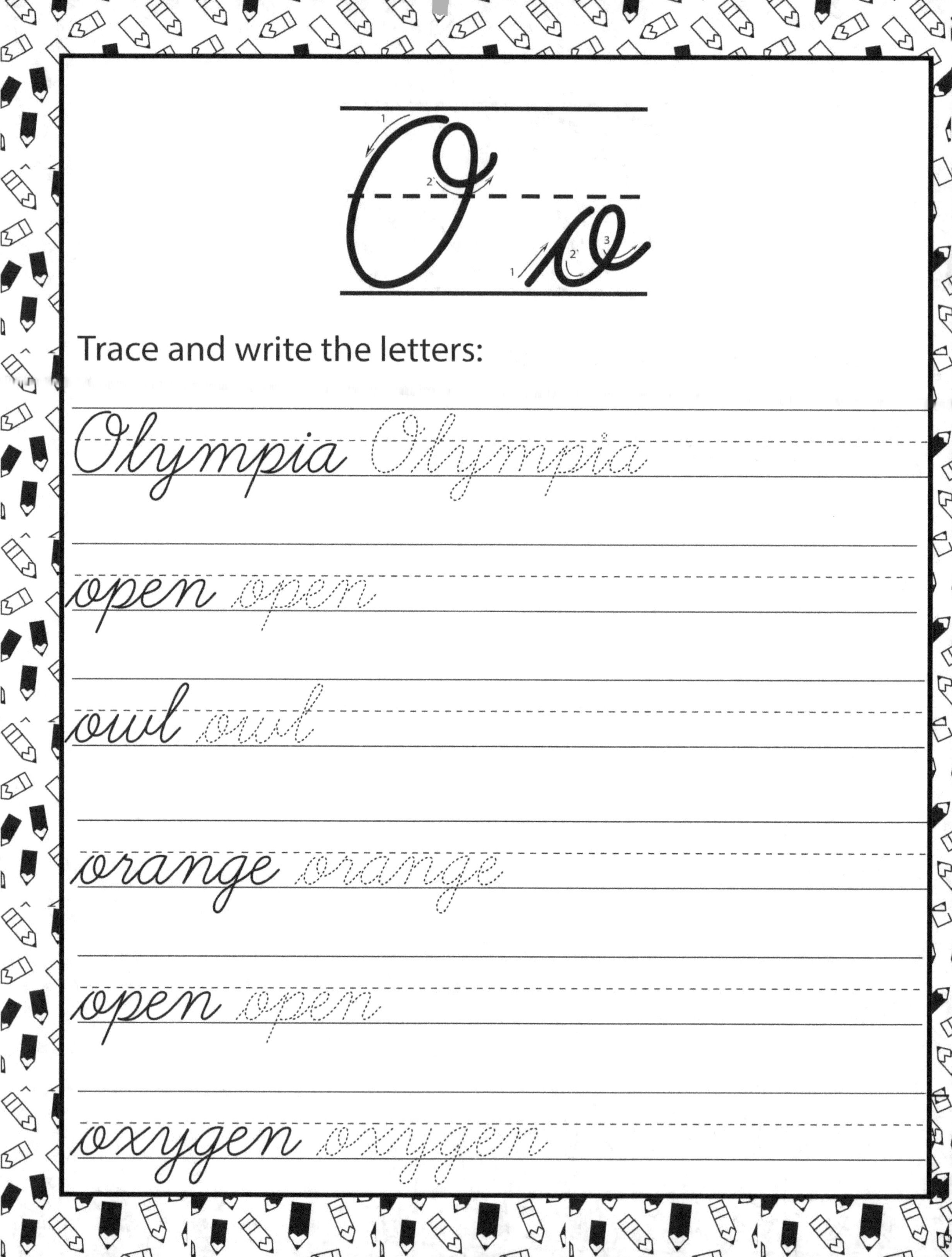
O o
1
2
1
2
3
Trace and write the letters:
Olympia Olympia
open open
owl owl
orange orange
open open
oxygen oxygen

Pp

1 2 1 2 3 4

Trace and write the letters:

please please

paper paper

picnic picnic

pair pair

people people

Paris Paris

Q q
1
2
1
2
3
4
5
Trace and write the letters:
quaint quaint
queen queen
quote quote
Quentin Quentin
quiz quiz
quarter quarter

Rr

Trace and write the letters:

rose rose

rabbit rabbit

road road

Roger Roger

ring ring

riding riding

Trace and write the letters:

sofa sofa

sand sand

song song

Spain Spain

since since

spell spell

Tt

Trace and write the letters:

tap tap

team team

trying trying

together together

their their

Tampa Tampa

Uu

Trace and write the letters:

under under

unite unite

until until

Utah Utah

uneven uneven

usual usual

Vv

Trace and write the letters:

vision vision

view view

very very

Venice Venice

visit visit

vowel vowel

Ww

Trace and write the letters:

water water

woman woman

wild wild

wolf wolf

West West

why why

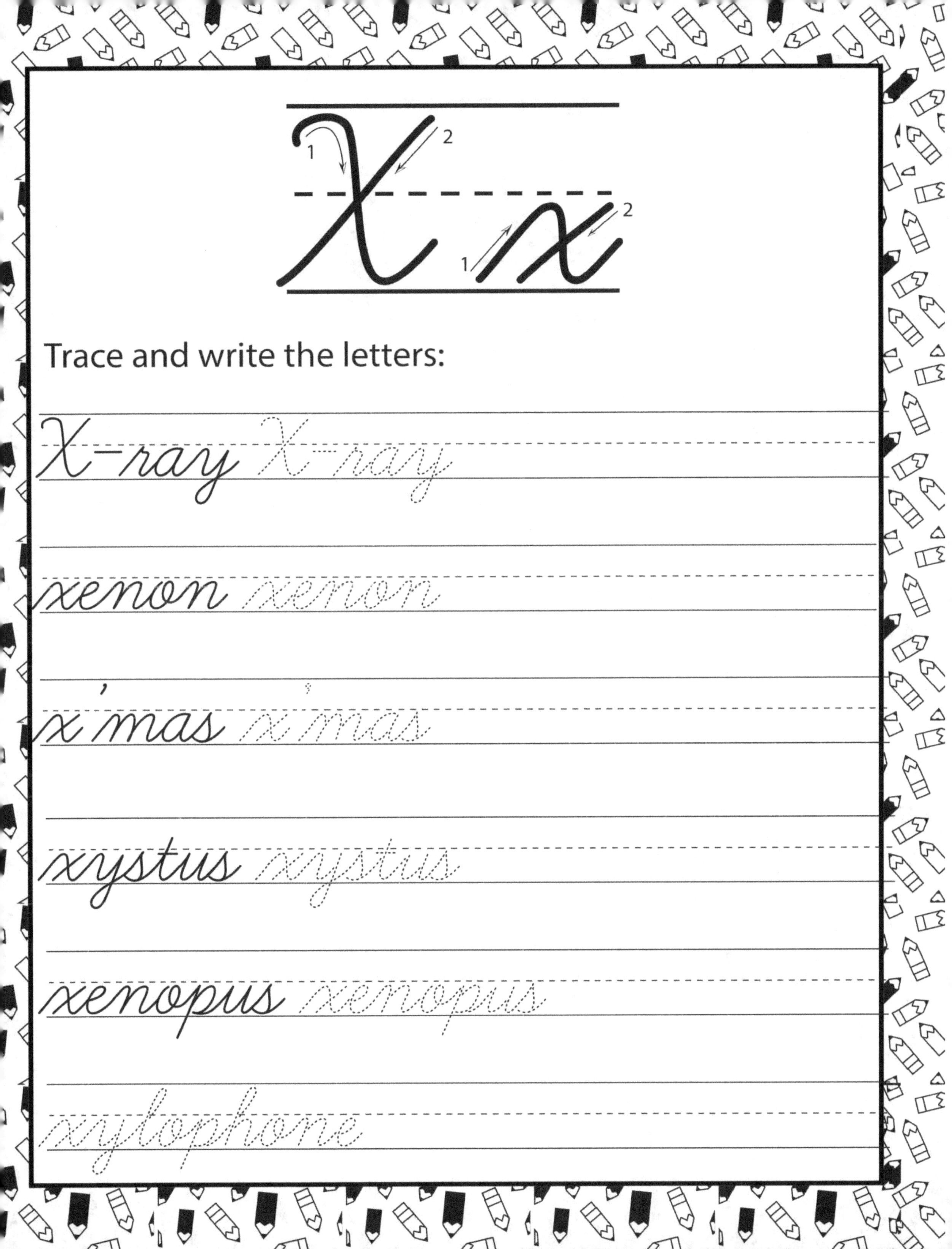

Xx
1
2
1
2
Trace and write the letters:
X-ray X-ray
xenon xenon
x'mas x'mas
xystus xystus
xenopus xenopus
xylophone

Yy

1 2 1 2 3 3

Trace and write the letters:

yellow yellow

yams yams

yarn yarn

yolk yolk

York York

yourself

Zz
1
2
1
2
Trace and write the letters:
zinc zinc
zoom zoom
zero zero
Zagreb Zagreb
zoo zoo
zebra

Cursive Sentences Worksheets

A penny saved is a penny earned

It's fun to do the impossible

Make each day your masterpiece

Honesty is the best policy

The truth is the strongest argument

A voice is a very powerful thing

A long trip begins with a single step.

To have a good friend, be a good friend.

Mistakes are proof that you are trying.

The first to apologize is the bravest

If you cannot be kind, be silent.

Welcome every morning with a smile

No act of kindness is ever wasted.

Success is dependent on effort.

All is well that ends well.

Health is better than wealth.

Life is what you make it.

You have to take the bitter with the sweet.

Hold a true friend with both your hands.

Keep your friendships in repair

To light a candle is to cast a shadow.

Learn as if you were to live forever.

Where there's a will, there's a way.

If at first you don't succeed, try try again.

BONUS Cursive Poems

Humpty Dumpty

Humpty Dumpty sat on a wall,
Humpty Dumpty had a great fall;
all the king's horses
and all the king's men
couldn't put Humpty together again

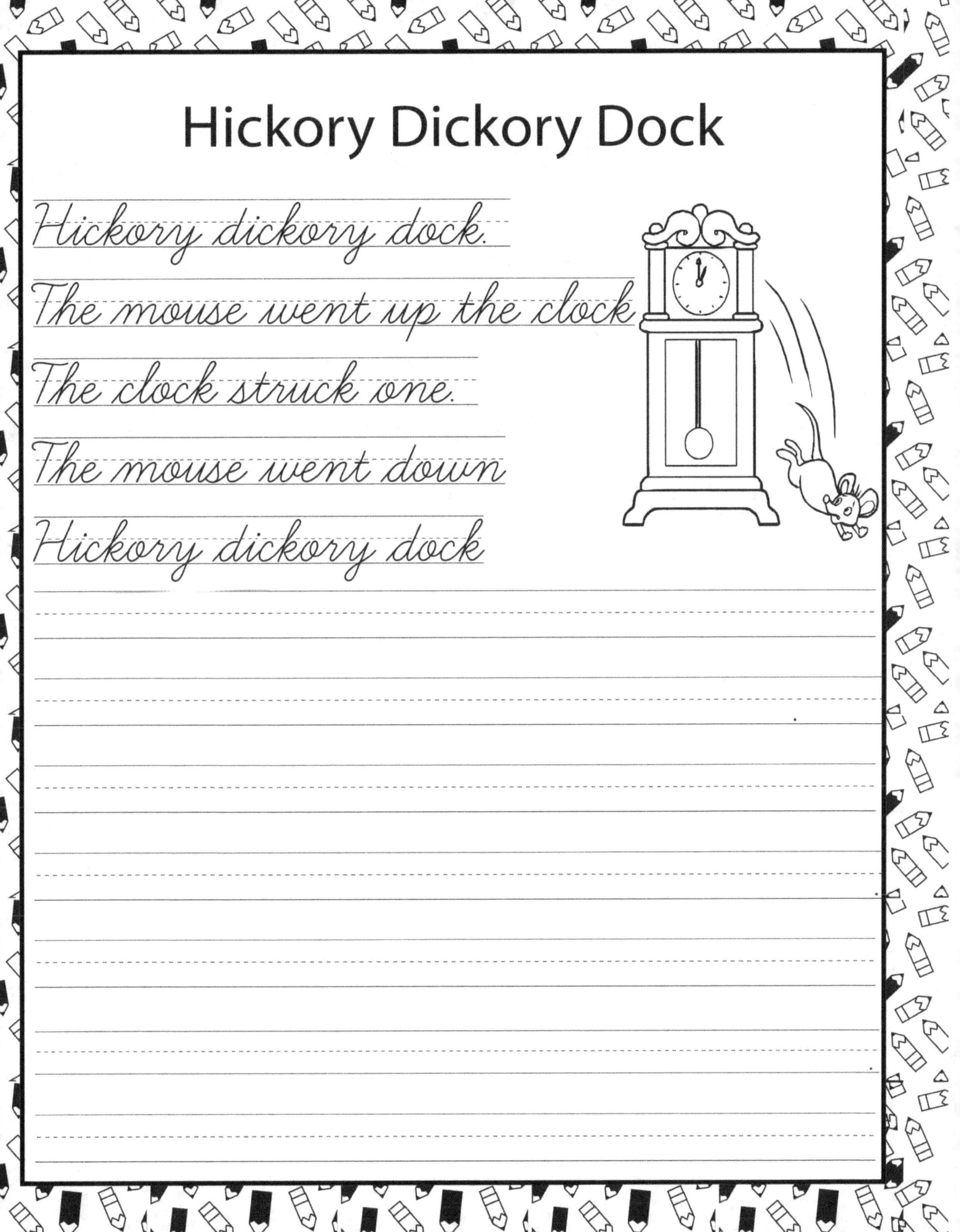

Hickory Dickory Dock

Hickory dickory dock.

The mouse went up the clock

The clock struck one.

The mouse went down

Hickory dickory dock

Jack and Jill

Jack and Jill went up the hill
To fetch a pail of water
Jack fell down and broke his crown
And Jill came tumbling after